POWER LIVING UNDER GOD

30 DAY DEVOTIONAL

FELICIA WILLIAMS

Copyright © 2021 Felicia Williams

All rights reserved.

Table of Contents

Shifting Your Focus 10
The Appropriate Response 12
Light in Darkness 14
Power in Weakness 16
Fear Not 18
His Peace for My Pain 20
Truth Downloading 22
Forward Living 24
Does Your Love Cover? 26
I Need a Charge 28
Beware of Imposters 30
PRESS 32
Why Pray? 34
A Place Called Home 36
Stay Synced 38
Let's Take a Selfie 40
A Closer Look 42
Surrender and Trust God 44
No Limits 46
I'm Not Alone 48
Small Beginnings 50
The Earth is The Lord's 52
Glory Revealed 54
It's Not Over Yet 56

Practice What You Preach 58
Shhh! Listen 60
Letting Go of Offenses 62
Do You 64
Running On Empty 66
I Was Chosen for This 68

THE
Power Living Under God

Dedication

This devotional is dedicated in memory of my father Billy, in honor of my mother Florence, to my children, Alante, Alexis, Azariah, and my grandchildren, Kayson and Ger'Moni.

May your lives shift toward an intimate relationship with God as you allow the power of His word to transform your lives for abundant living. This is our legacy: The Plug - Power Living Under God!

Acknowledgments

A special thank you to those who have lifted this project in prayer and with substance have continually given me words of encouragement. Your prayers and support were essential in taking this project from paper to purpose, from vision to reality. I am especially appreciative to:

Diane Wolford for your authentic and transparent relationship as a big sister and friend.

Victoria Davis for your prayers, words of encouragement, leadership, friendship, and guidance that pushed me into purpose.

Avis LaFrance for being my prayer and thought partner on the journey. Your prayers, support, and friendship are impeccable.

Dr. Stacia Alexander thank you for being my strategist in overcoming insecurities to promote the power within. You and the women of *The Emotionality of Success Strategy Cohort* provided the synergy needed for growth.

Gee J. Parks thank you for your patience, skill, and talents in getting my vision to reality.

Thank GOD THE FATHER, SON, AND THE HOLY SPIRIT.

I am The PLUG - Power Living Under God.

"I Am, I Will because I Can, said I to Myself as I rise above my old self to embrace my new self!

God has smiled on me, and He has set me free. He has been good to me!"

The PLUG (Power Living Under God)

Day 1

Shifting Your Focus

He continued, "Go home and prepare a feast, holiday food, and drink; and share it with those who don't have anything: This day is holy to God. Don't feel bad. The joy of God is your strength!"
Nehemiah 8:10 (Message)

    The experiences of anything or anyone new brings with it the good, bad, and ugly. As you accept this new thing, new day, or new way, check your focus. How long you feel sad or sorry for yourself is determined by your focus. To concentrate steadily on what's wrong is to remain distracted. Directing your attention to what is good, and right is to remember that you are precious in His sight, and this too will pass. Go ahead and process what you're feeling, then escape into the presence of God. In return, receive joy; His joy will be your strength.

Power Prayer

God, fix my eyes on what is right in all that is wrong. I am yours and you know all too well everything that I am experiencing. My feelings are real. Help me to live out my life in your strength by staying plugged into you. So Be It!

Reflections

_____
_____
_____
_____
_____
_____
_____
_____
_____
_____
_____
_____
_____
_____
_____
_____

The PLUG (Power Living Under God)

Day 2

The Appropriate Response

Know this, my dear brothers and sisters: everyone should be quick to listen, slow to speak, and slow to grow angry.
James 1:19 (CEB)

      The question we must ask ourselves before, during, and after every life encounter with people, places, and things is, "Do I respond, or do I react?" The world insists that we react rather than respond. Our reactions are influenced by our need for immediate control of a situation. This false sense of control is our defense against fear, guilt, and shame. Reacting brings a lot of stress, which can grow into anger and lead to outrage if left untamed; it becomes the poison we use to harm others knowingly and unknowingly. God desires that we choose the proper response over the negative reaction. Every answer must start with listening, followed by few words, to extinguish the rage or anger.

Power Prayer

God, bridle my tongue and open my ears to listen as I respond appropriately to life's situations and circumstances. So Be It!

Reflections

_____
_____
_____
_____
_____
_____
_____
_____
_____
_____
_____
_____
_____

The PLUG (Power Living Under God)

Day 3

Light in Darkness

God said, "Let there be light." And so light appeared.
Genesis 1:3 (CEB)

Have you ever been in a dark situation? Maybe you are there today. Darkness brings despair, disappointment, discouragement, and disengagement; all the ingredients needed for a recipe of hopelessness, and these are indicators that point to a despondent life.

In the beginning, there was darkness until light was created. Like our lives, in the beginning, we entered this world in darkness from our mother's womb until we were born in the light of Jesus upon our acceptance of Him and the finished work done on the Cross. Now, when we enter a dark place or space in our lives, we can call forth the light, and we can be the same light to others.

Power Prayer

God, light my world with your presence. Be the light in me and through me as darkness tries to overwhelm me. Let me shine in this dark world as I follow you as the light of the world. I am willing to stay plugged into your power that lights my way. So Be It!

Reflections

_____
_____
_____
_____
_____
_____
_____
_____
_____
_____
_____
_____
_____
_____

The PLUG (Power Living Under God)

Day 4

Power in Weakness

My grace is enough; it's all you need. My strength comes into its own in your weakness.
2 Corinthians 12:9 (Message)

The words power and weakness seemingly don't belong in the same sentence. It has been during my weakest hours in life that I've found my greatest strength. On our own, we are powerless. The world we live in teaches us that we are strong until we show signs of weakness, and then the world rejects and abandons us.

Thanks be to God that when we are weak, His power within us is made strong. Our weaknesses place us in a position to acknowledge our need for Him. It's okay to be weak so that God can flex His power in our lives.

Power Prayer

God, thank you for the weak moments and times in my life. The sufficiency of your grace in my weakness drowns out my need to be strong. I commit to staying plugged into your power as I depend on your strength in my weakness. So Be It!

Reflections

_____
_____
_____
_____
_____
_____
_____
_____
_____
_____
_____
_____
_____
_____
_____

The PLUG (Power Living Under God)

Day 5

Fear Not

Don't fear because I am with you; don't be afraid, for I am your God. I will strengthen you; I will surely help you; I will hold you with my strong righteous hand.
Isaiah 41:10 (CEB)

Google defines fear as "an unpleasant emotion caused by the belief that someone or something is dangerous, likely to cause pain, or is a threat." The verb form of fear is shown as "being afraid."

We all have been afraid or felt fear concerning someone or something in our lives. The emotion of fear is natural; it's our reaction to this feeling that causes us to live years of complacency, immobility, and missed opportunities. God doesn't want the emotion of fear to stop us from His divine plan for our lives. We must persevere, even in fear, trusting His provision. It has been said that fear is "False Evidence Appearing Real." Don't allow fear to override your faith to trust God. Without faith, it's impossible to please Him.

Power Prayer

God, give me the confidence to not be afraid, but to trust and believe you are with me. I am unplugging myself from living in fear. So Be It!

Reflections

_____
_____
_____
_____
_____
_____
_____
_____
_____
_____
_____
_____
_____
_____

The PLUG (Power Living Under God)

Day 6

His Peace for My Pain

Don't be anxious about anything; rather, bring up all of your requests to God in your prayers and petitions, along with giving thanks. Then the peace of God that exceeds all understanding will keep your hearts and minds safe in Christ Jesus.
Philippians 4:6-7 (CEB)

Right out the gate in this scripture, we are given a command: "Don't be anxious...." Interestingly, the word choice didn't include mad or sad. I believe the reason is beneath every emotion known to humanity lies the spirit of anxiousness. This feeling of uneasiness triggers other emotions, which can send us on an emotional rollercoaster.

Ending a 28-year marriage left me in a place of worry, but I was willing to take the risk of being talked about, lied about, hurt, and broken to make an honest trade with God; my weakness for His strength and pain for my purpose. I took my sorrow and hurt to God in prayer, and in exchange, I received His power to live again.

Are you willing to make a trade with God? What are you ready to exchange for the peace of God? God wants to make a deal with you. First, connect to Him to hear what you need to give up. He wants to trade your pain, hurt, disappointment, guilt, shame, regret, defeat, and failure for His peace. He is the Prince of Peace! I don't know about you, but I'm ready to give it all up for peace. Honestly, giving up isn't easy, but it's worth it. Make the trade today.

Power Prayer

God, grant me the peace to accept the things I can't control. Teach me to trust you with all my cares and concerns. I'm plugging into peace! So Be It!

Reflections

_____
_____
_____
_____
_____
_____
_____
_____
_____
_____
_____
_____
_____
_____
_____
_____

The PLUG (Power Living Under God)

Day 7

Truth Downloading

You must be doers of the word and not only hearers who mislead themselves.
James 1:22 (CEB)

Have you downloaded the newest app? Google Play and the Apple Store are the largest distribution channels with the most extensive number of apps available. Google Play for Android users has 2.7 million apps versus the Apple store, with 1.85 million available for its users.

Daily we are flooded with true and false information. We rely on apps for knowledge, food, music, and a host of other things, yet we don't trust God enough to take Him at His word. He has graciously inspired men to write down His words in 66 books. What God thinks about a matter is readily available to us in the truth of His word. To live an abundant life, we must download the word of God in our lives and live by it daily. God encourages you and me to become doers of His word, not hearers only deceiving ourselves.

If the only time you hear God's word is Sunday or on a YouTube channel, then you are robbing yourself of the power of God's word to change you from the inside. The word of God doesn't work until you have downloaded it into your daily living and stay connected to its POWER!

Power Prayer

God, help me to be a doer and not a hearer only of your word. I want to live out your truth in my daily life as long as I shall live. I'm choosing to stay plugged in so that your word can light my life! So Be It!

Reflections

_____
_____
_____
_____
_____
_____
_____
_____
_____
_____
_____
_____
_____
_____
_____

The PLUG (Power Living Under God)

Day 8

Forward Living

It's not that I have already reached this goal or have already been perfected, but I pursue it so that I may grab hold of it because Christ grabbed hold of me for just this purpose. Brothers and sisters, I don't think I've reached it, but I do this one thing: I forget about the things behind me and reach out for the things ahead of me. The goal I pursue is the prize of God's upward call in Christ Jesus.
Philippians 3:12-14 (CEB)

How many times have you set goals that seemed somewhat impossible to accomplish? The goals were made mentally but not written to visualize and execute so you never got around to completing them.

Did you know it's harder to unlearn something than it is to acquire new knowledge? Realize to move forward, there is no need to rehash what's behind you. Anticipating a future by reliving your past cannot be done. Perceiving what you've already been through as equal to what's ahead keeps the past and future balanced and no change in the direction. This state of equilibrium causes you to be at a standstill.

To practice forward living, you must forget the past and allow new things, new people, new thinking, new living, to come to be and press on. This will propel you to achieve greater insight, self-awareness, and the purpose of God's plan for your life. Are you willing to move in the process in order to grow to the next phase of your life? Are you willing to leave the past behind and press toward what awaits you in the future? If your answer is yes, then tell God you are ready and ask for His divine help. Try to go easy on yourself by not thinking too far ahead; take one day and one step at a time as you move into your destiny.

Power Prayer

God, you alone know what lies ahead of me into my future. Today, I surrender my past disappointments, pains, failures, loss, insecurities, fears, guilt, and shame into your hands. I accept the power within me to move forward to living the abundant life you have prepared just for me. So Be It!

Reflections

_____
_____
_____
_____
_____
_____
_____
_____
_____
_____
_____
_____

The PLUG (Power Living Under God)

Day 9

Does Your Love Cover?

Above all, have fervent and unfailing love for one another, because love covers a multitude of sins [it overlooks unkindness and unselfishly seeks the best for others].
Peter 4:8 (AMP)

Have you ever loved someone so much that it hurts? It seems like the more you love them, the more they hurt you. The love you give is not the love received, yet you continue to provide unconditional love.

God's love is supernatural. He loves us enough to look beyond our faults and cater to our internal needs. Now, demonstrating this kind of love toward those who have hurt us isn't easy. It takes uncovering the pain to acknowledge our true feelings. We must give what we feel in the moment a name: anger, hurt, frustration, betrayal, fear, etc., and then allow God to heal us over time. Once we go through the healing process, then we can love others past their faults and pain. Our need to be reconciled back to God supersedes our faults. His love covers us.

May you and I heal from our pain and love people where they are. Take the hurt to God in prayer.

Power Prayer

God, remind me that you loved me enough to send me your best in Jesus. Your love covers my faults, and I want to do the same for my family and friends. Teach me your ways and empower me to forgive and love others just as you forgive and love me. So Be It!

Reflections

_____
_____
_____
_____
_____
_____
_____
_____
_____
_____
_____
_____
_____
_____
_____

The PLUG (Power Living Under God)

Day 10

I Need a Charge

Why I ask myself, are you so depressed?
Why are you so upset inside?
Hope in God!
Because I will again give him thanks
my saving presence and my God.
Psalm 43:5 (CEB)

    Why is there a need for us to charge our mobile devices and our laptops? It's because the system is running slower than usual, or the battery is low. We are much like our electronics. We can run slower than normal when life happens, and we find ourselves in a dark place of depression. Our thinking becomes stuck, and we lose the physical, mental, emotional, and financial ability to move. We feel immobile and need a spiritual charge to rise above where we are to a place of hoping in God. We must change our perspective about ourselves and the circumstances we face to get the charge needed for the journey.

    Are you feeling depressed due to life's circumstances? If your answer is yes, try focusing your mind on God and who He is in your life. Be aware of God's presence to help you cope with life.

Power Prayer

God, refresh me in every way that I receive the power of your Holy Spirit to move me out of the place of depression and help me place my hope in you alone. Then, I will be able to rise above my past and current darkness into your marvelous light. So Be It!

Reflections

The PLUG (Power Living Under God)

Day 11

Beware of Imposters

Beware of false prophets, who come to you in sheep's clothing, but inwardly are ravening wolves.
Matthew 7:15 (ASV)

"Beware" is a cautious term often overlooked because it's not prevalent in everyday language. It is used occasionally when there is possible danger such as walking too close to the fence of homeowners with a vicious dog. A sign is placed there to warn us beyond what we may see or hear. If the sign has been read and not overlooked, this forewarning allows us to anticipate the risk and brace ourselves for the possible encounter.

I invite you to look at this scenario in a spiritual sense as you encounter countless people in your lives from season to season. Our consciousness leads us to beware, but we allow human external appearances to override people's internal motives. We are wise to judge the character as evidence of sheep or wolf identification. People can look nice on the exterior, but are vicious in their behavior, like a raving wolf. Sheep and wolves have common outer appearances: coverings (clothing), four legs (same mobility), yet their bite is different (motives).

The lesson we must learn is to examine the evidence of a person's life. It's important to recognize traits in destructive people by knowing what to look for: puffed up with pride, unloving, unforgiving, slanderous, and cruel (*2 Timothy 3:2-9*). Evil pretends to be good. It's easier to be a wolf in the church than it is in the streets.

Power Prayer

God, teach me to not naively close my eyes and think there are no wolves in my family, church, community, or mirror. Give me discernment to determine good from evil. May the spirit of truth lead me in all things. May I hate what you hate and love as you love progressively in and out of relationships. So Be It!

Reflections

_____
_____
_____
_____
_____
_____
_____
_____
_____
_____
_____
_____
_____
_____
_____
_____

The PLUG (Power Living Under God)

Day 12

PRESS

I press toward the mark for the prize of the high calling of God in Christ Jesus.
Philippians 3:14 (KJV)

Have you ever found yourself in a difficult relationship? You keep reaching out, being kind, doing the right thing, saying the right thing, being an active listener for things to get better between the two of you. My friends, this is called "pressing." Those of us who are willing to take positive action are intentional about moving the relationship in a new direction. Maintaining good relationships with family, friends, associates, mentors, therapists, etc. takes work. Our efforts determine the outcome of whether our relationships are healthy or not.

God desires an intimate relationship with each of us. He is persistent in His love toward us at all times. God presses upon our hearts and minds to follow Him, to listen to Him, to acknowledge Him in everything we do. He listens when we pray, bestows upon us new mercy every day, and is faithful in all His ways. His "pressing" is a desire for us to have an intimate relationship with Him. Our relationship with Him is a high calling and we must press to stay connected.

Power Prayer

God, help me to press into the power of maintaining a relationship with you through prayer, worship, serving, and giving so my connections with others will be rewarding. So Be It!

Reflections

_____
_____
_____
_____
_____
_____
_____
_____
_____
_____
_____
_____
_____
_____
_____

The PLUG (Power Living Under God)

Day 13

Why Pray?

> Pray without ceasing.
> I Thessalonians 5:17 (KJV)

Have you ever not felt like praying? Well, trust and believe that you are not alone. Yes, the struggles in life can be overwhelming that we begin to react instead of crying out to God in prayer. In other words, we are encouraged in scripture never to stop praying. Even when angry, mad, upset, excited, thankful, gracious, etc., we ought to always pray. Praying without ceasing means never stop! It means to pray as if your life depended on it because it does.

I live a lifestyle of prayer. I pray because I'm helpless. It doesn't change God; it changes me from the inside out.

Power Prayer

God, thank you for giving me the opportunity to communicate with you. There isn't a problem too big for you to solve. May I take the time to pray every day. Upgrade my communication with you from an activity or habit to a lifestyle. So Be It!

Reflections

_____
_____
_____
_____
_____
_____
_____
_____
_____
_____
_____
_____
_____
_____

The PLUG (Power Living Under God)

Day 14

A Place Called Home

Let us test and examine our ways and let us return to the Lord.
Lamentations 3:40 (AMP)

    Have you ever felt like you needed to get back home quickly, especially after being out of town for a lengthy period? Internally our mind, body, and soul can make us feel out of place and fill us with a need to call home. Many times, we have a longing to fill the void of discontentment by trying to find a way back to our foundation.

    Practically speaking, let's look at it this way. We all have mobile devices with a home page with easy access to applications that are essential to our likes and needs. Spiritually speaking, prayer, devotion, and studying God's word is our home page. It's there we find peace in midst of a chaotic world. In His presence is the fullness of what we need (*Psalm 16:11*). It's time to go back home.

Power Prayer

God, direct me to the home page in our relationship with you as the keeper of my soul. Help me stay connected to the power of your presence that will always lead me home whenever I stray away. Thank you for your direction. So Be It!

Reflections

_____

_____

_____

_____

_____

_____

_____

_____

_____

_____

_____

_____

_____

_____

The PLUG (Power Living Under God)

Day 15

Stay Synced

*Your word I have treasured and stored in my heart,
that I may not sin against You.
Psalm 119:11 (AMP)*

To hide something, one must have possession of it. You and I are not able to hold on to things we don't retain. Likewise, if we are not intentional about spending quality time with God by praying, reading, studying, and applying the truth of the written word daily, we become out of sync. This can include losing focus by paying attention to meaningless things rather than valuing what's important. People, places, and things can draw us away from our purpose, which is simply to bring God glory in our life story.

When we decide to include God in our schedules, agendas, and daily living, we connect to His presence and power. It is then that we can truly live consistent lifestyles that represent the divine kingdom.

Power Prayer

God, lead me to live a life that includes my time with you as a priority so that I may sin less. So Be It!

Reflections

_____
_____
_____
_____
_____
_____
_____
_____
_____
_____
_____
_____
_____
_____
_____

The PLUG (Power Living Under God)

Day 16

Let's Take a Selfie

Let's take a good look at the way we're living and reorder our lives under God.
Lamentations 3:40 (MGS)

Have you taken a selfie lately? In today's world, the answer to this question is probably a resounding yes! Technology now includes high-tech cameras for taking the best quality pictures.

Taking selfies seems to be a part of our daily lives. Once the photos are taken, we share them on social media for everyone to see. But sometimes we are so self-absorbed with our physical appearances that we neglect the internal reflection of who we are. We don't mind examining other's motives for their photos to determine if they measure up to our standards.

But, what about taking a selfie using the word of God as a camera and measuring our ways, behaviors, and attitudes strictly by His standard? This type of "internal selfie" would cause us to live selflessly and allow others to see God bigger. Others will be amazed by who He is and what He has done to enhance our ugly, sinful selves.

Power Prayer

God, take away my self-centeredness and allow my life to be a reflection of you as I examine myself by your work. So Be It!

Reflections

_____
_____
_____
_____
_____
_____
_____
_____
_____
_____
_____
_____
_____
_____
_____
_____

The PLUG (Power Living Under God)

Day 17

A Closer Look

Search me, O God, and know my heart: Try me, and know my thoughts; And see if there be any [a]wicked way in me and lead me in the way everlasting.
Psalm 139: 23-24 (KJV)

Do you have a BFF (Best Friends Forever)? Do you have a personal relationship with someone who you think knows you well? Certainly, we all have that one person we believe knows us best. I would challenge us by saying not even that person knows us to the extent that God does.

We don't know ourselves wholeheartedly. There are things deep within our hearts that we are unaware of, and if God doesn't reveal it, then it goes unexamined. When we don't allow God to take a closer look on the inside, we suffer the daily results of bitterness, unforgiveness, and resentment. A closer look by God allows for internal surgery to take place and begins our recovery from the inside out.

Power Prayer

God, take a closer look on the inside of me. Search me and remove anything that is stunting my growth and intimate relationship with you. I will keep still until you perform heart surgery on me. So Be It!

Reflections

The PLUG (Power Living Under God)

Day 18

Surrender and Trust God

And lift thou up thy rod, and stretch out thy hand over the sea, and divide it: and the children of Israel shall go into the midst of the sea on dry ground.
Exodus 14: 16 (ASV)

Have you ever felt surrounded by obstacles that keep you from crossing over to a new thing, new season, new life, new perspective, a new way of being and doing things? Are you experiencing this feeling of apprehension today? Well, I want to encourage you to surrender and trust God. Do it, even if you are afraid.

When we don't surrender, it places us in a fighting position. We are fighting against the will of God with our own will. We are left feeling oppressed by our stubbornness to surrender. The best choice is to submit for the best results. Choosing to trust God no matter what we think replaces our insecurities with faith in the One who can fight on our behalf as we cross over the red sea of our lives. He will safely get us to the other side.

Power Prayer

God, deliver me to the other side of my journey as I stretch forth into my future, trusting you to lead me every step of the way. So Be It!

Reflections

_____
_____
_____
_____
_____
_____
_____
_____
_____
_____
_____
_____
_____
_____
_____

The PLUG (Power Living Under God)

Day 19

No Limits

Jesus looked at them and said, "With man, this is impossible, but with God, all things are possible."
Matthew 19:26 (CSB)

I can think of several situations, incidents, or scenarios where I believed the outcome would be impossible. Often, we think of impossibilities more than we realize or verbalize. The reality is we are finite; therefore, it takes faith in supernatural powers to believe what is impossible.

God has no limits; He is a limitless exclamation and specializes in making those impossible things possible. Let us take our eyes off what we can see in the natural and fix our eyes on the author and finisher of our faith *(Hebrews 12:2)*, Jesus! It is by faith and not by sight that we encounter the limitless power of God working in our lives. Take the restrictions off God and watch Him do the impossible when we trust and believe that He can do it.

Power Prayer

God, help my unbelief. Help me to see beyond what I see with my natural sight. So Be It!

Reflections

_____
_____
_____
_____
_____
_____
_____
_____
_____
_____
_____
_____
_____
_____
_____

The PLUG (Power Living Under God)

Day 20

I'm Not Alone

Even though I walk through the valley of the shadow of death, I will fear no evil, for you are with me; your rod and your staff, they comfort me.
Psalm 23:4 (NASB)

Today loneliness is an epidemic all over our land. People of all walks of life are experiencing the sadness of being alone. Even those in a marital relationship can feel a great sense of loneliness.

Why? It's our need to be connected; it's natural. We thrive when we live in a community and engage with others. But when we are not content in a divine relationship with God, the spirit of loneliness often consumes us. Jesus felt alone in the garden of Gethsemane until He surrendered His will to the Father.

Power Prayer

God, help me to give myself totally to you so that loneliness doesn't consume me to death. You sacrificed on the cross so that I may live. So Be It!

Reflections

_____
_____
_____
_____
_____
_____
_____
_____
_____
_____
_____
_____
_____
_____

The PLUG (Power Living Under God)

Day 21

Small Beginnings

Who [with reason] despises the day of small things (beginnings)? For these seven [eyes] shall rejoice when they see the plumb line in the hand of Zerubbabel. They are the eyes of the God which roam throughout the earth."
Zechariah 4:10 (AMP)

Have you started yet? If not, now is the time to begin whatever you've procrastinated about. Once you begin a "BIG" thing with a small effort, God can cause it to grow enormously. An oak tree started as an acorn. God took something small, increased, and expanded its potential beyond the physical state. Another example is human life. Our conception as an embryo grows and develops for approximately nine months until birth. The change from a baby into an adult is extraordinary.

As you start a new business, new goals, new visions, and new dreams, discouragement may try to hinder you; don't let it. Talk back loud and clear. Do not despise these small beginnings because my God rejoices in the fact that you have begun, and He will bring it to completion. Be encouraged. Get started today!

Power Prayer

God, thank you for the small beginnings in my life. Help me not to discount the things I have started, but to believe with your help I will finish strong! So Be It!

Reflections

_____

_____

_____

_____

_____

_____

_____

_____

_____

_____

_____

_____

_____

_____

The PLUG (Power Living Under God)

Day 22

The Earth is The Lord's

The earth is the God's, and the fulness thereof; the world, and they that dwell therein.
Psalm 24:1 (KJV)

Planet Earth is the only planet where life can exist. When was the last time you thought about the planet we live on? Maybe you never considered or contemplated long about the existence of earth, but its beauty and complexity are simply amazing.

When was the last time you went on vacation? Did you take the time to reflect on the beauty of nature? Doing so causes us to see how great the Creator of the universe really is. Reflections bring a greater sense of awareness about God.

After taking a flight over the ocean, I was awakened in amazement by God's majesty. The Divine is incomparable to anyone or anything. This is His land and we are His people. We owe gratitude to the Creator for His generosity and creativity that allows us to reap daily benefits. This land was made for you and me.

Power Prayer

God of creation, I honor you today as I reflect on your goodness in nature. May your beauty show up in my life as I witness it outside in our environment. So Be It!

Reflections

_____

_____
_____
_____
_____
_____
_____
_____
_____
_____
_____
_____
_____
_____
_____

The PLUG (Power Living Under God)

Day 23

Glory Revealed

Jesus answered, "Neither hath this man sinned nor his parents, but that the works of God should be made manifest in him.
John 9:3 (KJV)

Have you ever looked at your life or the life of another and became amazed at the magnitude of strength being displayed? Does it amaze you how God shows himself to be strong in human weaknesses? When our finite collides with God's infinite power, it is Glory revealed.

This also happens when life greets us without warning through life-threatening diseases, the sudden death of a child, senseless murders, natural disasters, tragedies, and more uncertainties. As we struggle with our reality, we come face-to-face with God's sovereignty. We are powerless but God is all-powerful. It's like strength on steroids through the frailty of being. These experiences cause us to reflect on our human nature compared to God's omnipotence. It leads us in the worship of the one and only wise God.

Power Prayer

God, thank you for your reality experiences that reveal your amazing Glory in my story. So Be It!

Reflections

_____

_____

_____

_____

_____

_____

_____

_____

_____

_____

_____

_____

_____

_____

_____

The PLUG (Power Living Under God)

Day 24

It's Not Over Yet

We are troubled on every side, yet not distressed; we are perplexed, but not in despair; persecuted, but not forsaken; cast down, but not destroyed.
2 Corinthians 4:8-9 (KJV)

Have you ever experienced pain, disappointment, heartache, challenges, tears, anger, struggle, hopelessness, desperation, exhaustion, or anxiety? I'm sure your answer is a resounding yes! Truly if you have lived, you have experienced some of these emotions. I certainly have. Sometimes all these feelings may occur at once.

I was in a place of loneliness that didn't feel good but thanks to God's presence, I overcame this feeling. The good news is that the loving voice of God is always quietly saying to our spirits, it's not over yet. My lonely place resulted from a failed marriage of 28 years. My marriage ended, but God spoke the plans He had for me *(Jeremiah 29:11)*. God still had work for me to do and that work was in me. He is doing an inside-out job. And thank God, I don't look like what I have been through.

Be encouraged and believe that God is saying the same to you; it's not over. It's okay to feel these emotions. Go through the process and be patient with yourself as God has been with us. He is faithful and will never leave you.

Power Prayer

God, when I'm tired, weak, and worn out, lead me into your presence where I can hear you whisper to me it's not over yet. May I receive that truth from your word and trust you to watch over it if I live this truth. So Be It!

Reflections

The PLUG (Power Living Under God)

Day 25

Practice What You Preach

They claim to know God, but they deny God by the things that they do. They are detestable, disobedient, and disqualified to do anything good.
Titus 1:16 (CEB)

    We don't need another sermon preached more than we need it practiced. We all have heard, "practice makes perfect." The truth is practice makes better, not perfect. Our "talk" should align with our "walk." Living out God's truth is more impactful to unbelievers than merely speaking it. If what I say doesn't line up with what I do, it's all in vain.

    The world today is filled with many words being shared on social media. We read more positive or inspirational posts, text messages, and quotes than we read the truth in God's word. Although we are ingesting the text, very few of us are living it. It all just sounds good and makes it look as if we are good people. But the more we preach or talk without practicing, the more we deceive ourselves. We are just like dead men walking.

Power Prayer

God, help me to not just be a hearer of your word but also a doer. When my walk doesn't line up with what I say by your spirit, prompt me that I may exhibit behavior and a lifestyle that will be pleasing unto you. Practicing your truth will make me a better me. So Be It!

Reflections

_____
_____
_____
_____
_____
_____
_____
_____
_____
_____
_____
_____
_____
_____
_____
_____

The PLUG (Power Living Under God)

Day 26

Shhh! Listen

... and thine ears shall hear a word behind thee, saying, this is the way, walk ye in it; when ye turn to the right hand, and when ye turn to the left.
Isaiah 30:21 (ASV)

Have you ever been confused about which way is the right way? Is this person right for me? Am I doing the right thing? Should I stay or should I leave? Am I at the right job? Am I in the right profession? Did I make the right decision? Do I have the right attitude? Questions, questions, questions. Our minds are filled with them day in and day out until we cannot silence our souls.

Once we quiet our inner being, we can hear the voice of God giving us clarity for decision making. Listen carefully and be encouraged. If you went left when you were supposed to go right, it's okay. God's grace is sufficient, and He will lead us back to the right way and the right things. He is the way, the truth, and the life.

Power Prayer

God, anoint my hearing so I will hear your voice leading in the right direction for my life. Speak God; I'm listening. So Be It!

Reflections

_____
_____
_____
_____
_____
_____
_____
_____
_____
_____
_____
_____
_____
_____

The PLUG (Power Living Under God)

Day 27

Letting Go of Offenses

Good sense and discretion make a man slow to anger, and it is his honor and glory to overlook a transgression or an offense [without seeking revenge and harboring resentment]
Proverbs 19:11 (AMP)

    Are you offended by what someone has said or done to you? If so, I want to encourage you not to take offense as stated in scripture. It makes good sense that we don't allow what others do or not do get in the way of what God is doing.

    Oftentimes, we stop our own progress because we allow ourselves to be moved or bothered by what family, friends, and yes, even our enemies say about us. It is time we stop hearing others and listen to God. We need selective hearing from without and active listening from within. If what others are saying isn't in alignment with what God says, we can delete, disregard, and reset.

Power Prayer

God, help me to be slow to react and quick to hear from you. Give me the power to resist being offended. Enable me to overcome evil with good. For you have said it is an honor and glory for me to overlook without revenge what others have said or done. If they've done it to me, they've done it to you. I have the power to overcome offenses. So Be It!

Reflections

_____
_____
_____
_____
_____
_____
_____
_____
_____
_____
_____
_____
_____
_____
_____

The PLUG (Power Living Under God)

Day 28

Do You

Whatever you do [no matter what it is] in word or deed, do everything in the name of the Lord Jesus [and in dependence on Him], giving thanks to God the Father through Him.
Colossians 3:17 (AMP)

    Stop! Re-read the scripture above. Notice the second and third words: "you do." This verse makes no reference to what other people do but the actions by you and me. Often, we are more concerned about other people instead of ourselves. Whatever we find ourselves doing, we should do it all in the name of Jesus.

    Take a closer look in the mirror. Once you can identify with yourself, you can start living your best life in words and deeds. God designed each of us uniquely with gifts and talents. After the process of being trained, nurtured, corrected, and matured by the word you can apply it for abundant living. You can be and do what God desires. Be encouraged and just do you!

Power Prayer

God, teach me to depend on you to help me be the best I can be individually to collectively change the world. So Be It!

Reflections

_____
_____
_____
_____
_____
_____
_____
_____
_____
_____
_____
_____
_____
_____

The PLUG (Power Living Under God)

Day 29

Running On Empty

He refreshes and restores my soul (life); He leads me in the paths of righteousness for His name's sake.
Psalm 23:3 (AMP)

Are you running on empty? Many times, we move about our day even when we are tired and weary. Our sluggishness can be caused by poor eating habits, restless nights, and mental overload. Also, if allowed, people can drain the very strength out of us. This can be subconscious or intentional. Whatever the case, we can walk around depleted from within and need a spiritual boost to continue the journey.

In times like this, we need to position ourselves in a quiet place to meditate on God's word and listen as He speaks. God desires to fill the empty places of your heart, mind, and soul. We must take time to rest and be restored as God did in *Genesis 2:2*: *By the seventh day God had finished the work He had been doing so on the seventh day He rested from all his work.*

Power Prayer

God, teach me how to spend my time daily, weekly, monthly, and yearly completing the assignments you have for me. Fill me up God with your Holy Spirit that I might pour into others. So Be It!

Reflections

_____
_____
_____
_____
_____
_____
_____
_____
_____
_____
_____
_____
_____
_____

The PLUG (Power Living Under God)

Day 30

I Was Chosen for This

"For many are called (invited, summoned), but few are chosen."
Matthew 22:14 (AMP)

The word "chosen" can be defined in the dictionary as one who is the object of choice or divine favor, an elected person. As we reflect on the meaning of the word, it should change how we use it about ourselves. What have we been chosen to do?

As God's chosen people, we carry out assignments with power until we take our last breath. Chosen people usually hold positions without titles long before their assignments are visible to the public. An example is David, a shepherd boy who tended sheep but became king and pastored God's people.

Chosen individuals have been endowed with supernatural power to carry out difficult challenges and tasks. Being chosen comes with a price. The cost of being chosen can be measured in suffering, disappointment, joy, pain, sunshine, and rain. The amazing truth about being chosen is that He who began a good work in you will carry it on to completion until the day of Christ *(Philippians 1:6).*

Power Prayer

God, thank you for choosing me to carry out your plan for my life! So be it!

Reflections

www.ingramcontent.com/pod-product-compliance
Lightning Source LLC
Chambersburg PA
CBHW050706160426
43194CB00010B/2022